Rebecca Faulkner | **How to get ahead in**

Engineering & Design

Raintree

www.raintreepublishers.co.uk
Visit our website to find out more information about **Raintree** books.

To order:
Phone 44 (0) 1865 888113
Send a fax to 44 (0) 1865 314091
Visit the Raintree bookshop at **www.raintreepublishers.co.uk** to browse our catalogue and order online.

First published in Great Britain by Raintree, Halley Court, Jordan Hill, Oxford OX2 8EJ, part of Harcourt Education.
Raintree is a registered trademark of Harcourt Education Ltd.

Editorial: Melanie Waldron, Lucy Beevor, and Kate Buckingham
Design: David Poole and Calcium
Illustrations: Geoff Ward
Picture Research: Ruth Blair and Maria Joannou
Production: Huseyin Sami

Originated by Chroma Graphics
Printed and bound in China by South China Printing Company

10 digit ISBN 1 406 20441 2
13 digit ISBN 978 1 4062 0441 4

11 10 09 08 07
10 9 8 7 6 5 4 3 2 1

British Library Cataloguing in Publication Data
Faulkner, Rebecca
Engineering and Design. - (How to get ahead in)
620'.002341
A full catalogue record for this book is available from the British Library.

Acknowledgements
The publishers would like to thank the following for permission to reproduce photographs: Alamy Images pp: **32** (Alan King), **4** (David Robertson), **19** (QA Photos); Construction Photo Library p. **14** (Paul McMullin); Corbis pp: **27** (Bernard Annebicque), **50** (Julian Martin/EPA), **11** (Michael Prince), **8** (Ricardo Azoury), **26** (Schlegelmilch), **48** (The Cover Story), **12** (Helen King), **46** (P. Winbladh/Zefa), **16** (Steve Lupton); Getty Images pp: **15** (Stone/ Keith Wood), **31** (Stone/ Michael Rosenfeld), **35** (Stone/ Rod Morata); Harcourt Education pp: **30**, **51** (Tudor Photography); Nokia p. **38**; photos.com p. **20**; Puma.com p.**10**; Report Digital p. **37** (Paul Box); Rex Features pp. **6** (Brian Smith), **34** (Herbie Knott), **13** (James D. Morgan), **21** (Sipa Press), **9** (Colin Galloway), **24** (Paul Cooper); Science Photo Library p.**17** (Maximilian Stock Ltd).

Cover photograph of plane turbine, reproduced with permission of Getty Images/Imagebank.

Contents

Words appearing in the text in bold, **like this**, are explained in the glossary.

The world of engineering

What do you imagine when you think of a career in engineering? Do you see yourself sitting at a computer, designing bridges or mobile phones, or working in a huge factory operating a machine that assembles cars? These are just a few of the hundreds of different careers in the engineering industry. Finding the information you need to help you decide which career is right for you can be difficult. It is very important to find the career that suits you so that you will be happy in your job. That is where this book comes in. It will introduce you to the engineering industry, explain what types of job it offers, and help you work out if it's the industry for you.

below: *The Forth Road Bridge in Scotland, built over 100 years ago, was a huge engineering project. It is still an icon of great engineering.*

This book cannot tell you everything about the engineering industry, it can only give you an introduction. Some sources of further help are listed at the back of this book, on page 52. To find out about the organizations that interest you, you will need to visit their websites or write to them. You can also get advice from your careers advisor at school. They will be able to help you choose a career that is right for you.

The engineering industry is very much affected by new technology. This is because advances in technology affect how things are made, what is made, and therefore what engineers do. Today most engineering and design involves using computers. Engineers who used to perform repetitive tasks in factories now supervise **robotic** machinery to do the same tasks.

Engineering is an exciting industry to work in, as it is constantly changing. This also makes it a challenging and demanding career, but one that can also be very rewarding. Imagine seeing something that you have designed or helped to build actually in use by thousands of people.

WOMEN AT WORK

Engineering employs approximately two million people in the UK. You may think that most engineers are men, but nearly 15% of engineering students are women. Women work in all areas of engineering, from operating machines in factories to designing aircraft to building bridges.

Are you interested in how and why things work? Are you good at science and maths? Are you good with your hands? Do you enjoy problem solving? If so, a career in engineering could be for you. The skills of engineers are needed everywhere, and engineers are very much in demand. In fact, in many areas of engineering there are shortages of people with the necessary skills. All of this is good news for you if you are thinking about a career in engineering.

Chapter 1

What is the engineering industry?

Before we go any further, let us think clearly about what engineering actually means. What do you imagine when you think of engineering? Do you picture someone in greasy overalls mending a car in a garage, or do you imagine a team of people building a huge shopping complex? Engineering is a lot more than this. Everything you use in your daily life involves engineering. The fridge and washing machine in your home, your MP3 player and your mobile phone, and the computers you use at school were all designed and built by engineers.

BY DESIGN ...

Engineering is the process of designing and making the machines we use in our everyday lives. All engineering involves design. Make a list of all the items you use in a day that are designed and built by engineers.

left: *James Dyson designed and built the Dyson vacuum cleaner.*

A diverse industry

The engineering industry involves a wide range of activities, from sitting at a computer, designing a **microchip** for an iPod, to finding faults in trains, to operating a drilling machine in a factory making aircraft. It is all about designing and making things, and is at the forefront of technological change. Engineers are involved in researching, designing, making, and using the latest techniques and equipment. As we will see in this chapter, there is much more to it than mending cars and building things.

The range of careers in the industry is immense. In fact, there are so many options that it is often difficult to know where to start. The five main types of engineering are:

- **mechanical engineering**
- **electrical engineering**
- **electronic engineering**
- **civil engineering**
- **chemical engineering.**

Other types of engineering include materials engineering (designing and making new materials), biomedical engineering (designing and making machines and equipment for hospitals), aeronautical or aerospace engineering (designing and making aircraft), agricultural engineering (designing and making farming equipment), mining and petroleum engineering (designing the processes for **extracting** minerals and oil and converting them into useful products), and marine engineering (designing and making machinery for use in ships and shipyards).

In order to begin to find out if a career in engineering is for you, you need to decide which area of engineering interests you. The five main sectors of the engineering industry are described on the pages that follow. As you read each description, think about which sector or sectors are more appealing to you than the others.

above: *All of the machinery in this car production line has been carefully designed and engineered.*

Mechanical engineering

Mechanical engineers design and make any kind of machinery or equipment that has parts that move. This can range from the nuts and bolts that are on your bike to cars and space **satellites**. As a mechanical engineer you could find yourself working in TV broadcasting, space travel or medical science – to name but a few areas of work. Approximately 20 per cent of all qualified engineers are mechanical engineers.

Electrical engineering

When we look at the everyday things in our lives it is hard to find anything that does not require electricity in order for it to be made or for it to work. Electrical engineers are involved in electricity generation on a large scale, and usually work in power stations. This means they produce and control the electricity we use in our everyday lives to heat our homes, light up street lamps, and drive trains. There has been a shortage of skilled electrical engineers in the UK for many years, so if you are looking for a career in this area your skills should be in demand once you qualify.

Electronic engineering

When you look at a mobile phone or a DVD player it is hard to imagine how it works. An electronic engineer is the person who designed and made it. Electronic engineers are involved in electricity generation on a small scale. They work with **circuit boards** and create the tiny impulses of power that make your mobile phone, computer, DVD player or iPod work. If you have a brilliant idea for the next generation of mobile phones then a career in electronic engineering could be for you.

Civil engineering

Civil engineers design and build structures you will find in the built environment all around you, for example bridges, houses, roads, **dams**, airports, and even schools. As a civil engineer you will first design a structure, taking into consideration its strength, **form,** and **function**. You will then decide what materials should be used to build it, such as steel, concrete, brick or wood. You have to make sure that the structure remains safe for the length of its intended lifetime.

Chemical engineering

Chemical engineers design and develop a whole range of products, from petrol to cleaning agents. They apply their knowledge of maths and chemistry to solve problems and create new materials. The material that some of your clothes are made of will have been designed and made by chemical engineers. As a chemical engineer you could be working in the oil and gas industry, the **pharmaceutical** industry, the medical industry or the chemical industry itself.

We have looked at the main areas of the engineering industry. Now we can look at specific jobs that you could do within this diverse industry.

above: *Amazing structures like this – the Taipei 101 tower in Taiwan – have very complex designs.*

Get ahead!

A good way to find out more about the different types of engineering is by looking at university **prospectuses** or websites. Here you will find information about coursework in the different areas of engineering. This will help you work out which type is more suited to you.

Chapter 2

What types of jobs are there?

The engineering industry offers a huge range of jobs, from aircraft technician to heating engineer, to welder, to electronic design engineer. Opportunities for work exist throughout the UK, and there are jobs at all levels: management, professional, skilled, and semi-skilled. Within each branch of engineering there are five main types of job:

- professional or **chartered** engineer
- technical or incorporated engineer
- engineering technician
- craft engineer
- machine operator.

Each job is different, and every person has different expectations about what they want to achieve in their career.

left: *Design includes how well something fits in with current fashions as well as how it performs.*

Read through the following jobs and try to decide if any of them appeal to you. If they don't, this does not mean a career in engineering is not for you. This is just a small selection of the vast array of possible jobs that exist within the industry.

Professional or chartered engineers

Professional engineers work on the design, development, manufacture, and sale of new products and materials. You would be working at the forefront of technology, using the latest techniques to solve engineering problems and make decisions. You could also manage other staff, for example, you might be a team leader who is responsible for the performance of your team.

above: *As a chartered engineer some of your time will be spent creating accurate designs and plans.*

Chartered civil engineer

Civil engineers work alongside architects. They ensure designs for structures such as buildings and bridges are safe and they choose the appropriate materials for building them. You would be expected to supervise and manage the construction of your design. There would be a lot of variety in your job – one day you might be on site, supervising builders, the next in the office at your **drawing board**. You need to be creative in order to design imaginative structures, and also **analytical** to make sure that the structure will be safe. You would probably work in a team, supervising and advising other members of staff, so you would have a thorough understanding of whatever project you are working on.

Technical or incorporated engineers

Technical engineers carry out a wide range of technical activities under the guidance of professional engineers. They identify and solve problems and make decisions based on their experience. As a technical engineer you would work closely with others and inform other members of your team about your ideas and solutions to problems.

Technical electronic engineer

As an electronic engineer you would need to be involved in researching, designing, and developing new electronic products such as computers or MP3 players. You would work as a member of a team, supervised by a professional engineer. Whichever project you are working on, for example, designing a new microchip for a digital camera or researching the possibilities for more advanced mobile phone transmissions, you would need a thorough understanding of the whole project, as you are likely to be managing other members of your team.

below: *Electronic engineers often work at computers to design and develop new products.*

Engineering technicians

Engineering technicians are also problem solvers, but carry out fewer activities than technical engineers. They work in all aspects of engineering and normally work as part of a team, together with craft, technical, and professional engineers.

Aeronautical engineering technician

As an aeronautical technician you would be working on one aspect of the design, repair or manufacture of aircraft. You would work in a specialized unit, and your work could include repairing engines or manufacturing aircraft parts. You would work as a member of a team, but you would be responsible for your own work. You would be supervised by a technical or professional engineer.

CAD draughtsperson

Computer Aided Design (CAD) enables engineers to see a **3D** model of the product before it is made. A CAD **draughtsperson** uses a CAD system to produce these 3D engineering drawings and instructions. These are used by other engineers to create the products in the drawings. You would therefore need to have a good understanding of engineering drawings and an eye for detail in order to be a draughtsperson. Due to recent advances in CAD technology there is a shortage of CAD draughtspeople in the UK, so this is a good area to consider for a career.

above: *Aircraft need to be designed, created, and maintained by very skilled engineers.*

Craft engineers

Craft engineers turn ideas into products. They are able to interpret engineering drawings and instructions and use their practical skills to produce what is required. As a craft engineer you would need to be able to operate a number of handheld and **power tools**. You might specialize in one type of engineering, or provide general services across the whole spectrum of the engineering industry.

Welder/sheet-metal worker

A welder bends and joins pieces of metal together using special techniques. A sheet-metal worker uses hand tools to bend, cut, fold, and join different metals to create products or components.

Maintenance fitter

Fitters work in many different areas of engineering, including electrical, mechanical, and aeronautical. They maintain and repair industrial machinery and equipment in factories.

left: *Craft engineers interpret drawings and operate tools to get the job done.*

Machine operators

Machine operators work at the heart of the production process. Their jobs might include product assembly (putting a product together); operating machines such as drilling machines, grinding machines, **lathes** and cutting tools; finishing work such as spraying or polishing; and inspecting work for faults. Some jobs are repetitive and easy; others are more demanding.

Get ahead!

1. Find out about three more jobs in the engineering industry and list the main duties for each.
2. Visit www.totaljobs.com and search for jobs under the heading "engineering, manufacturing, utilities". Are there any you would like to do?

Assembler

An assembler works on an **assembly line** in a factory. An assembly line is like a giant conveyor belt. As an assembler you would work on one area of the assembly line, operating a machine that puts together one part of a product before it moves on to the next machine on the assembly line. The work is likely to be very repetitive, but you need to be able to keep concentrating so you do not make mistakes. Assemblers are needed in all types of factories producing all sorts of products. You could be assembling anything from cars to electric kettles to furniture.

below: *The people who operate huge drills like these need to understand how they work so they can operate them safely.*

Chapter 3

What will the working environment be like?

Do you prefer to work in a large, open-plan office, or do you need your own quiet space to concentrate? Do you like to know what you have to do each day, or do you like surprises? In this section you will begin to get an idea of the working environment you can expect for jobs in engineering.

You need to think about you career choice carefully. Different people want different things from their careers. You may want:

- a challenge
- a lot of money
- the opportunity to meet lots of new people
- a chance to be part of a team
- to work 9 to 5 rather than long hours
- a chance to develop your skills.

Most people want to work in the engineering industry because they enjoy finding out how things work or enjoy using their hands to operate tools.

MAKE A LIST

- List the things you want from your career.
- List the type of work that interests you.
- List the things you definitely don't want to do.

right: *Is making lots of money important to you? This could influence your choice of career.*

Working conditions

Working conditions vary, you may be working in an office, spending a lot of time in front of a computer screen or at a drawing board. You may be based on site, overseeing construction of a building or the installation of new equipement. You could be working for an organization of any size, from a huge open-plan office in an electronic engineering company, to a car factory, to a small workshop or laboratory where you may be working with just one or two others. Some of your work might involve travelling to visit clients. This could be in the UK or abroad, and may involve overnight stops. In most areas of engineering there are excellent opportunities for working abroad.

The type of environment you work in will depend on your chosen area of engineering, the type of products being produced or repaired, and the tools being used. Some working areas will be hot, noisy, and dirty, such as factories. Some may be cramped, such as small workshops where the work is very much hands-on, for example, repairing cars. Other places, such as chemical engineering laboratories, will be clean and the environment will be controlled very carefully, as you are likely to be dealing with hazardous chemicals. You may need to wear protective clothing on a daily basis.

below: *Many engineering jobs will be based in offices, working on plans and designs on computers using CAD programmes.*

above: *Protective clothing is essential if you are working in hazardous environments.*

CASE STUDY

James is a trainee electrical design engineer.

I work in an office with a team of designers, designing air conditioning systems for buildings. The team consists of a team leader, two mechanical engineers, and a CAD engineer. I spend a lot of time sitting at a drawing board or at a computer using a CAD system to check our ideas will work in practice. I also have a lot of meetings with other members of the design team and with the engineers who are actually making the items we design. I don't spend all my time in the office, though. I sometimes have to visit sites to see the layout of a building before I start designing systems for it. I may also need to visit a site during the building process if problems arise. I sometimes have to travel long distances, as we operate all over the UK.

Other areas of engineering can be also be dangerous, for example, you could be using large, heavy machinery on a worksite or in a factory, working underground in a mine, or working offshore on an oil rig. If you are an electrical engineer working in a power station you need to pay attention to your own safety and that of the people you work with at all times.

A typical working day

In general, for most jobs in the engineering industry you will work normal office hours, from 9.00 a.m. to 5.00 p.m., Monday to Friday. You will, however, be expected to work longer hours at busy times when project deadlines are approaching. Some machine operator jobs may require you to work shifts, as the machinery may operate 24 hours a day.

below: *Many commercial machines, like this drilling machine, are so expensive that they need to be running 24 hours a day to get the best value from them.*

left: *The best people to tell you about a typical working day in the engineering industry are those who work in it.*

CASE STUDY

Ashley is a repair development manager for an aerospace engineering firm.

I usually work 7.30 a.m. to 5.00 p.m., Mondays to Fridays. If the work is behind schedule I will sometimes have to stay later to get the work done. I work in an office in a test building and oversee a team of ten technicians, who dismantle and check aircraft engine parts. They then repair them and put them back in the aircraft or replace them. If any problems arise I am there to assist and advise.

CASE STUDY

Deeta is a technical services manager for a chemical engineering firm.

For me every day is different – that is what I like about my job. I work as part of a team of engineers and spend most of my day problem solving. I usually work in the office and start the day by answering calls and email queries about our products and solving problems for clients. The work involved in dealing with these problems can take all day, as I often need to discuss the queries with other team members.

I travel to Europe quite frequently to visit industrial sites and factories where I have meetings with clients or train new members of staff. I give presentations, usually to small groups of engineers. In total I probably spend about 3 months of the year travelling. I enjoy this a lot, but it can be tiring if I have to go on a lot of trips in a short space of time. I speak French and Spanish, which is definitely an advantage in this line of work.

CASE STUDY

Yasmine is an electronic design engineer.

My work is entirely office based, sitting in front of a computer, usually writing ***code*** *or solving problems with code I have previously written. Once a week I will have a meeting with the other members of my team to discuss how a project is progressing. I also do a lot of work liaising between customers and design engineers, which involves a lot of travel, mainly to the Far East. My working hours are relatively flexible and depend largely on how much work I have on. I usually work an 8- or 9-hour day, but may need to work longer hours when an important deadline is approaching. My department is about 90% male, but this does not bother me at all. I enjoy my working environment as the people I work with are great fun. I also find it very exciting that I am working at the cutting edge of technology – there is always something new to learn.*

below: *You can often earn much bigger salaries if you agree to work abroad for some companies. This petroleum engineer is working in the desert in the Middle East.*

How much will I get paid?

For some people, this is the most important question when deciding on a career. The good news is, engineers are in demand, which means salaries are often good. Having said that, rates of pay very a lot according to the specific job you do, where you work, the size of the company, the extent of your experience, and the type of qualifications you have. Some examples are given below.

Professional or chartered engineers

Professional engineers in mechanical, civil, electrical, electronic, and chemical engineering can expect to start on around £18,000 to £23,000 per year after graduating from university. With experience this can rise to £25,000 to £40,000 per year. Highly skilled mechanical, civil, electrical, and electronic engineers can earn up to £50,000, whereas senior chemical engineers can earn up to £90,000 per year.

Engineering technicians

As an apprentice you are likely to be paid around £10,000 per year. Once qualified, engineering technicians can expect to start on £15,000 to £16,000 per year. This can rise to £21,000 with experience, and senior technicians can earn upwards of £30,000 per year.

Craft engineers

Salaries for craft engineers can vary hugely, but you can expect to start on £9,000 to £10,000 per year. After a lot of experience you could expect your salary to rise to between £13,000 and £18,000 per year. In some types of engineering, with relevant experience and qualifications, it is possible to earn £20,000 to £30,000 per year.

Machine operators

How much you earn as a machine operator will depend on the product and the company you are working for. You can expect to earn between £10,000 and £20,000 per year.

Chapter 4

Am I the right person for the job?

You will know by now that there are many different types of jobs in engineering, attracting many different types of people, so it is difficult to pinpoint one set of skills that you will need whatever job you are applying for. You will find there are opportunities for many different types of people. In this section we will look at the main personal qualities and skills that might be useful for jobs in this industry. As you read the information, think carefully about your own personality and your likes and dislikes.

Communication skills

You need to have strong communication skills, both written and spoken. This is because you will need to be able to get your ideas across clearly to others. You will also need to be **persuasive**, as sometimes you will need to persuade other people that your ideas are good or prove that they will work. At school you will have plenty of opportunities in your English lessons to develop these skills, and it is very important that you do. You will also need to write reports and be able to make presentations to small or large groups of people. When you are asked to do research for homework, you can practise these skills.

CASE STUDY

Kim is an aeronautical engineer.

Technical skills are important in this industry, but you also need to be able to communicate effectively with those around you. Much of the work I do is team-based, so you have to be able to get on with people and work together in order to get projects finished on time. If there is a breakdown in communication it affects the whole team and makes it difficult to work efficiently. You also need to have an enquiring mind and enjoy solving problems, as there are always plenty of engineering problems in my day-to-day working life.

Problem-solving skills

Engineering is all about finding solutions to problems, so you need to be good at problem solving and also enjoy it. For example, you may have to research and understand complicated numerical information, use your skills and knowledge to analyse it, and think of solutions to any problems that you find. You will therefore need an enquiring and analytical mind, and should enjoy finding out how things work.

above: *At the high end of engineering, the product not only has to work perfectly, but has to look modern and striking too.*

Creativity and design skills

As an engineer you need to be creative, practical, have a good imagination and be able to pay close attention to detail. You need to have the ability to constantly develop new ideas, new products, and new ways of doing things.

As an engineering technician or craft engineer you will be using tools and materials such as wood, metal, and chemicals to create things. You therefore need to enjoy using your hands for practical tasks such as making or repairing things. You will often have to use your **initiative** to provide creative solutions to problems.

As a draughtsperson you will need to have a good eye for detail and be very accurate in your work. As a craft engineer you have to accurately interpret drawings so you will also need an eye for detail as well as patience, as it may be painstaking work.

CASE STUDY

Robin is a marine engineer.

Apart from engineering skills and experience, a problem-solving mind is essential for my job. I think that problem solving forms a large part of your job whatever type of engineering you go into, so if you are no good at it then maybe this is not the career for you. You also need to be open to new ideas and able to adapt to new situations. Due to advances in technology the engineering industry is continually moving forward, and to keep pace with this I have to adapt to the change and the new problems it brings, otherwise I will be left behind. I supervise a team of engineers and therefore need to have strong leadership skills. This means I need to have good general knowledge of all the engineering disciplines so I can communicate effectively with all types of engineers.

above: *You will need to keep up-to-date with the latest technologies to become a successful mechanic. These engineers are monitoring racing car statistics during a Grand Prix.*

Technology skills

As an engineer you will often be working at the forefront of technological developments. This means you need to be adaptable and able to cope with a job that may change. Information technology (IT) is important in the engineering industry, so you need to have good IT skills. You will also need to be good with numbers for a lot of jobs in the engineering industry. Therefore, if you work hard and do well in your Maths and IT lessons you could be on track for an engineering career.

Teamworking skills

As well as having individual skills, you will need to be able to work well as part of a team. Most engineering jobs involve people with different skills working together as a team, so if you don't work well as part of a group this may not be the career for you. Sometimes, however, you will be expected to work on your own, and at times you will need to use your initiative to make decisions.

Other skills

For many senior jobs in the engineering industry you need to be able to cope with long working hours. Engineers in managerial positions need to have strong leadership skills so they are able to encourage workers to work well, both individually and in a team.

As many engineering firms have offices all over the world, you may have the opportunity to work abroad. In this case language skills will come in useful, so it is a good idea to work hard in your language classes at school. Also, for some engineering jobs, particularly those in electrical and chemical engineering, you need full colour vision, and some companies may need you to pass a colour-blindness test.

right: *As an engineer you can see your ideas turned into reality. Marc Mimram designed the Solferino footbridge in Paris.*

Finding the best career for you involves matching your skills and personality to the skills needed for a particular job. The best way to do this is to start by taking a close look at yourself. Are you good at problem solving? Are your communication skills strong? Do you work well in a team? Are you creative and imaginative? There is no point in applying to work as an electronic engineer if you can't stand working with computers.

SKILLS CHECKLIST

1. Fill in the checklist of skills below. Look back at the information in this chapter to see if your skills match up with those required by jobs in the engineering industry. Can you identify any area of the industry that you are particularly suited to?

Skills required	**Yes (✓)**	**No (✓)**	**Especially important for:**
Good communication skills	☐	☐	All engineering jobs
Good analytical skills	☐	☐	Professional engineer
Good with numbers	☐	☐	All engineering jobs
Good IT skills	☐	☐	All engineering jobs
Good at problem solving	☐	☐	All engineering jobs
Work well in a team	☐	☐	All engineering jobs
Creative and practical	☐	☐	Craft engineer
Eye for detail	☐	☐	Draughtsperson
Adaptable to change	☐	☐	All engineering jobs
Leadership skills	☐	☐	Professional engineer

2. Draw a table with the following headings:

- IT skills
- Team working
- Problem-solving skills
- Communication skills

Under each heading write down the things you have done that show you have these skills.

So, do you think you are the right person for a career in engineering? If you enjoy science and maths, are good at problem solving, can work as part of a team, and think you can cope with the challenges of new technology you are on the right track.

Chapter 5

What qualifications do I need?

Now you know what kind of person would be best suited to working in the engineering industry, but what qualifications do you need?

Engineering is an industry where it is possible to start from the bottom and work your way to the top. You can therefore start training as an engineer straight after your GCSEs or S-grades through a **Modern Apprentice** scheme. If you stay on at school to do A-levels, **National Vocational Qualifications** (NVQs), or **Scottish Vocational Qualifications** (SVQs) you will have more choice. You will then be able to go on to study for a recognized qualification, either through training at work or by taking a full-time course at university. This will give you a wider range of career opportunities and better chances of **promotion**.

There are a whole range of qualifications that can help prepare you for entry to engineering jobs, ranging from GCSEs, NVQs/SVQs and A-levels through to degrees and postgraduate qualifications. You need to think about what you want to do within the industry. Then you can decide which qualifications are most suitable.

For the jobs given over the next few pages, there is no single entry route. The qualifications described are the most common and most relevant for the particular job, but are by no means the only qualifications you could consider.

WHAT'S ON OFFER?

- NVQs and SVQs – These are more practical and less academic than A-levels. They provide a flexible approach to studying a number of different subjects and allow you to progress at your own pace. They have been developed to prepare you for a variety of jobs. You can gain NVQs/SVQs by taking a full-time course at college or you can study part-time while at work.
- Modern Apprenticeships – These provide an opportunity to develop skills and expertise and gain engineering NVQs/SVQs while at work.
- **Higher National Certificates** (HNCs) and **Higher National Diplomas** (HNDs) or degree courses – Many universities and colleges offer certificate, diploma, and degree courses in engineering and other related subject areas. Examples include HNDs in Applied Physics, and degrees in Mechanical, Civil, Electrical or Electronic Engineering.

Professional or chartered engineer

Professional engineers usually need a university degree in a relevant branch of engineering, such as civil, mechanical or electrical engineering. To get into a degree course you will need at least five GCSEs (grades A–C) and three A-levels (including Maths and a science, usually Physics or Chemistry). IT or Computer Science will be useful for electronic engineering, and it is also useful to have language skills. If you do not have A-levels it is possible to gain entry into an engineering degree by taking a foundation course. These are offered by universities and take 1 year to complete.

It may be also possible to become a professional engineer by progressing from a more technical level, but you will have a much better chance if you have a university degree.

CASE STUDY

Peter is a mechanical engineer.

I took the direct route into engineering. I did A-levels in Maths, Physics, and German before obtaining a degree in Mechanical Engineering. During my degree course I spent one year at a university in Germany, which gave me valuable experience of living in another country. Part of my course involved a work placement at a mechanical engineering firm, so I also had experience of working in the real world before I applied for my first job after graduation.

left: *There are many different engineering and design courses all around the UK. The tricky part is selecting which one to take!*

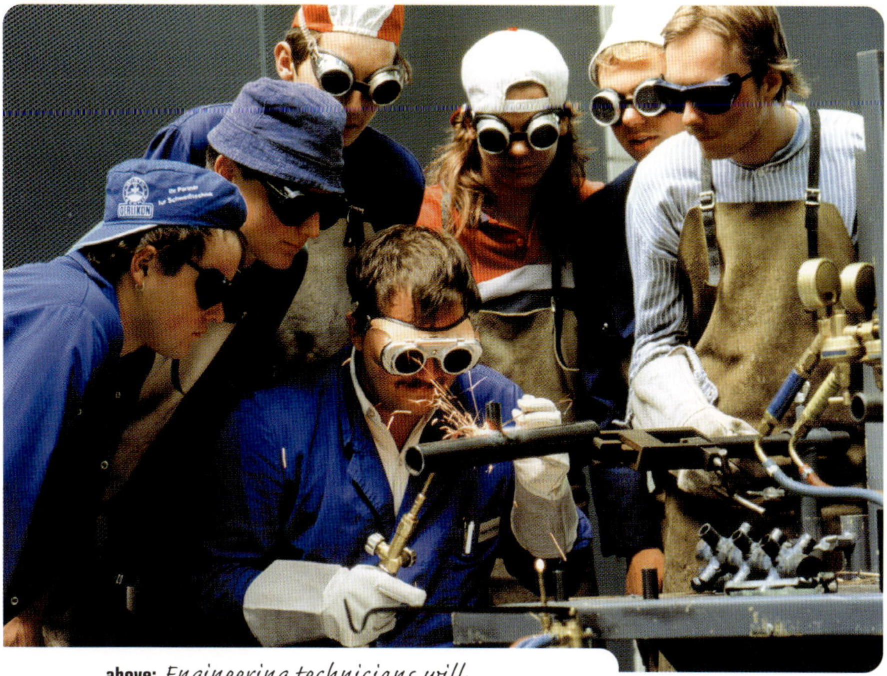

above: *Engineering technicians will learn many different skills.*

Technical or incorporated engineer

To become a technical engineer you will need an HNC/HND. To get on to a full-time university course you will need at least one A-level and four GCSEs (grades A–C). You could also work towards an HNC/HND part-time while you are employed as an engineering technician.

Engineering technician

To enter the profession at engineering technician level you will need an NVQ/SVQ in a related subject, for example Aircraft Maintenance Engineering, Installing and Commissioning Electrotechnical Systems, and Equipment or Engineering Assembly. There are different ways to go about this. You can either obtain an NVQ/SVQ through full-time study at college or you can enrol on a Modern Apprenticeship scheme. If you choose full-time study you will need a minimum of four GCSEs (grades A–C) or S-grades (grades 1–3), including English, Maths, and Science. If you undertake work-based training through a Modern Apprenticeship this takes 3 or 4 years. During this time you will gain valuable practical experience as well as working towards your NVQ/SVQ. If you take this route you will also get paid while you learn.

CASE STUDY

Sarah is in her fourth year of a Modern Apprenticeship at a nuclear power plant.

I was accepted on a Modern Apprenticeship straight after my GCSEs. For the first two years I learned different engineering skills on the job. I then had a variety of jobs repairing equipment and working with craft engineers on site. I also worked towards my NVQ. It would have been possible for me to stay in full-time education to gain NVQs, but I would have missed out on all the practical experience I gained as an apprentice. Safety is a big issue here, so I have also been on lots of safety courses and have to wear protective clothing at work. I have now started working towards an HNC and after that I hope to get on to a degree course to become a professional engineer.

below: *Nuclear power plants, like this one at Sizewell in Suffolk, employ skilled engineers to run the plant efficiently and safely.*

Craft engineer

It is not always necessary to have formal qualifications to become a craft engineer, and there are a number of possible routes you can take. If you have GCSEs in English, Maths and Science, you can apply for a 2-year Modern Apprenticeship programme. This includes work-based training and study towards an NVQ/SVQ.

If you choose, you can progress to the level of engineering technician if your apprenticeship is extended for a further 2 years. Alternatively, you can enter your chosen area of engineering at machine operator level and then progress to training as a craft engineer.

Machine operator

There are no specific qualifications needed to become a machine operator, but you may have to pass a selection test. GCSEs or S-grades in English, Maths and practical subjects will be useful. You can also become a machine operator through a Modern Apprenticeship scheme.

One thing you should note is that qualifications alone are no guarantee of a job in the engineering industry. A lot depends on your personality, attitude, communication skills, and having a common-sense approach to work and life in general.

Chapter 6

A foot in the door

You have excellent problem-solving and analytical skills, enjoy working in a team, and are good with numbers and computers. You seem like the ideal candidate for a position in the engineering industry ... but how do you go about actually getting a job?

Do well at school

Whatever job you are applying for in the engineering industry, most employers look for a good standard of secondary education, including GCSEs (A–C)/S-grades (1–3) in English, Maths and Science. This will be a minimum requirement, and while there are opportunities for school leavers to enter Modern Apprenticeships, for more senior jobs in this industry you will need a university degree in an engineering-related subject.

Maths skills will be important in any job that you do. Most jobs in the engineering industry will require you to work with numbers. As a civil engineer, your maths skills will be useful for calculating optimum sizes of structures. Mistakes are not an option, as if you get it wrong the building may fall down or the bridge may not be able to hold as much weight as you planned.

below: *Some designers and engineers can get it wrong. The Millennium Bridge in London was opened on 10 June 2000. It wobbled so much that it was shut 2 days later! Engineers had to work on correcting this fault and it was finally reopened in February 2002.*

Good English skills will be needed for writing formal letters and reports and for sending information round to work colleagues. If you have to speak to groups as part of your job, your oral presentation skills also need to be good. Other subjects such as History and Business Studies will give you useful communication skills as well.

You will also need to be good at science to work in the engineering industry. Physics is important for most branches of engineering. For example, as a civil engineer you will need to understand how forces impact on structures so the buildings that you design remain standing.

below: *A good understanding of maths will go a long way in engineering.*

Chemistry is necessary for chemical engineering as you need to know how different materials and chemicals act under different circumstances. Biology is central to biomedical engineering, as you need to understand how the human body works in order to design machines and instruments for use in treating patients.

For most jobs in the engineering industry you will be using a computer. You therefore need competent IT skills. Foreign languages, such as French, German, Spanish or Italian, are useful in firms with offices all over the world and may open up opportunities for you to work abroad.

The importance of work experience

A relevant qualification will be vital to your employment prospects. However, another key factor that employers will be looking for is work experience. There are plenty of types of work experience you can do while you are still at school or college that could improve your chances of getting into your chosen career.

Stacking shelves at a supermarket develops skills in stock control and teamwork. Routine office work in any office will develop your ability to deal professionally with colleagues. These are all things employers will be looking for.

Some engineering firms offer **internships** that you can do during your summer holiday. During this placement you may be work-shadowing someone. This involves following a member of staff to see what they do in a typical working week. It may also include work on an actual project, where you receive some sort of training. Competition for internships is often strong, so you will need to be prepared to work hard to get one. It is often a way in to the company, as if you impress your employers during your internship they may want you to join the company.

Not only is work experience important for impressing employers, it also gives you the chance to find out if the career you are thinking of is actually the one you want. You may have your heart set on working as a mechanical engineer, but when you actually start work you may find it is not really for you. Any work experience, whether it is a placement organized by your school or part-time work you have organized yourself, will give you an idea of working life and what the job itself is like.

above: *Getting an internship is a fantastic way to build up work experience.*

Once you have completed your work experience, you should think about what you got out of it and make a note of this. Describe any new skills or experiences that you gained, such as problem solving, using your initiative to tackle unfamiliar tasks, working in a team, relating to people you don't know, adapting to a new environment, following instructions or making presentations. It will also strengthen your communication skills to give a presentation about your work experience to your class. This could be as an oral presentation or a written report, or preferably both.

Having some experience of the world of work under your belt will show employers that you are keen and have made an effort to find out about work before applying for a job. It will also make you appear more confident, due to the extra knowledge and skills you will have gained.

Chapter 7

How to stand out from the crowd

Although engineers are in demand, getting a job in the engineering industry will not be easy. There will be lots of enthusiastic, highly qualified young people competing for a limited number of jobs. It is therefore not enough to have the relevant qualifications and work experience, you need to stand out from the crowd.

Employers usually look for a broad range of personal skills, including being able to work well in a team, being self-motivated, having good communication skills, and being good at problem solving. Think about what skills you have to offer, and spend some time finding out about the companies you would like to work for.

Job ads

To find out what jobs are on offer in the engineering industry you can search in a number of places.

- Look in newspapers, both local and national, for job adverts.
- Talk to your careers advisor at school.
- Visit the careers section of your local library.
- Look for the names of companies that you might be interested in working for on the Internet and in brochures. You can then write to them to see if they have any suitable work.
- Search the Internet for jobs. For example, totaljobs.com
- Visit job centres and recruitment agencies.

above: *If you are fascinated by the technology behind modern electronic gadgets, find out what the companies that produce them look for in their employees.*

Maintenance Engineer

Salary: to £32,000

Working nights, Sunday to Thursday (37.5 hrs per week), you will be responsible for the maintenance of a range of machinery and equipment. It is essential that you are a multi-skilled electro-mechanical engineer with previous maintenance engineering experience.

In return we offer ongoing training for your own personal growth and development. If this position is of interest then please in the first instance forward ... rent CV.

ENGINEERING SITE MANAGER

Salary: Negotiable

We require an experienced site manager for a 12-month project in the Netherlands.

Typical day-to-day tasks:

- Directing and planning the work team of 10.
- Providing weekly progress reports.
- Resolving drawing and construction problems on site.

Experience required:

- in-depth civil engineering experience.
- Excellent communication skills.
- Ability to interpret engineering drawings.
- Flexibility to work additional hours as required.
- A persuasive team-player with excellent problem-solving skills.

This is an exceptional opportunity for the right candidate offering superb rates of pay coupled with a fantastic benefits package. If you wish to be considered please respond to this advert today.

left: *Local and national newspapers are great places to look for job ads.*

Senior Lift And Escalator Engineer

Salary: Competitive Remuneration (including bonus and pension)

An engineer is required for a major programme of new installations and refurbishments on the underground rail network.

Main tasks:

- Provide engineering design leadership and guidance while acting as a positive role model for design team staff.
- Work with a team to resolve technical problems
- Identify creative design solutions

You will have at least 10 years engineering design management experience within the lift and escalator industry. You will be degree qualified, with chartered status.

Completing application forms

When you apply for a job, you will either have to fill in an application form or provide a CV. Whichever method you use, this will be the first impression the employer gets of you, so you need to get it right.

If the employer sends you an application form you must use this to apply for the job. The first thing you should do is photocopy the form, so you can create a rough draft on the photocopy. This way, if you make any mistakes, it does not matter. Read through all the questions before you start, and then take your time to fill in the answers. Make sure you answer the questions actually asked and always be honest in your answers. If you make things up, the chances are you will be found out if you make it to the interview stage.

Once you have checked your form for spelling mistakes, grammar, and punctuation, you can copy it onto the original application form. Keep your writing neat and tidy, and check the form again before sending it off, or better still get someone else to check it for you. Make sure you post it well before the closing date, and use a suitable envelope. Do not fold your application form. Keep a photocopy of it in case you get an interview and need to check what you wrote.

Before you fill your form in, it is very useful to try and work out what the employer will be looking for. Write down everything you think they will want to see evidence of on your application form. Then write down the skills you have that would be relevant to those required by the employer. They might be things you have done in school projects, your work experience or one of your hobbies.

HAVE A GO ...

Copy out and fill in the application form on the opposite page, using as many of the following phrases as possible. They are all things employers will like to see on your application form.

- Enthusiastic
- Hard working
- Good at writing and speaking clearly
- Honest
- Good at working in a team
- Reliable
- Willing to learn.

below: *You may be sent an application form like this when you apply for a job.*

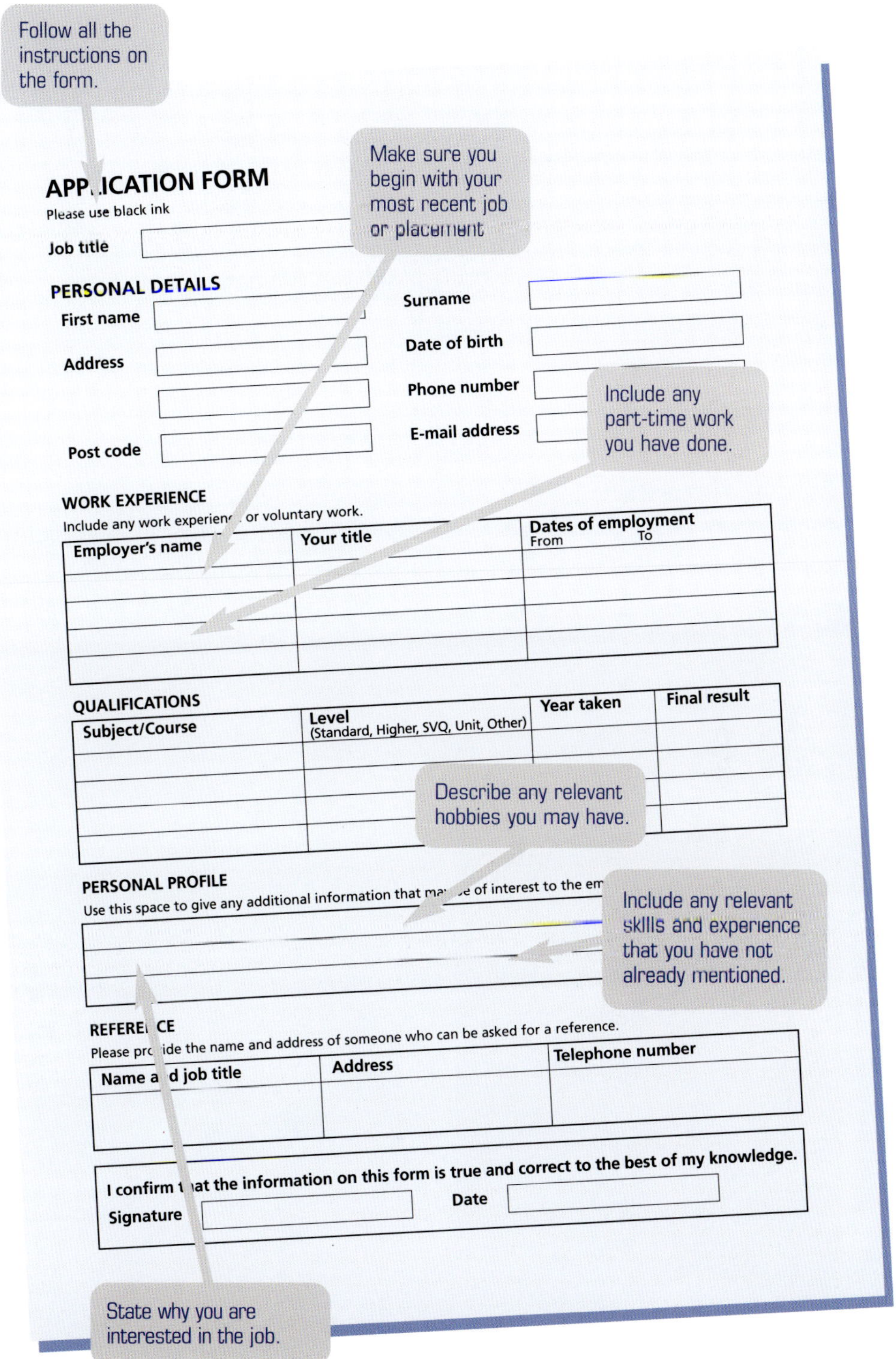

APPLICATION FORM

Please use black ink

Job title

PERSONAL DETAILS

First name | Surname

Address | Date of birth

Phone number

Post code | E-mail address

WORK EXPERIENCE

Include any work experience or voluntary work.

Employer's name	Your title	Dates of employment From	To

QUALIFICATIONS

Subject/Course	Level (Standard, Higher, SVQ, Unit, Other)	Year taken	Final result

PERSONAL PROFILE

Use this space to give any additional information that may be of interest to the employer.

REFERENCE

Please provide the name and address of someone who can be asked for a reference.

Name and job title	Address	Telephone number

I confirm that the information on this form is true and correct to the best of my knowledge.

Signature | Date

Your Curriculum Vitae

A curriculum vitae (CV) is a form that tells employers about your education, experience, and interests. Some employers will ask for a CV instead of sending you an application form to fill in. When you write your CV you will need to include all the information that the employer would have asked you for on an application form. You will also need to send a covering letter explaining why you are applying for the job.

An example of a CV is shown on the opposite page. It has been typed and has a clear layout. It first gives your personal details, such as your name, address school, etc. It then describes your qualifications, work experience, and interests. Try not to include too much information on your CV, as this will make it difficult to read (it should not be more than two pages long). You will need to stress all your good points on your CV, but you must be honest. If you play netball for your school team do not be tempted to exaggerate and say you play netball for England. If you get an interview, you will be asked lots of questions about what is on your CV, so if you exaggerated anything you will soon be found out. Once you have created your CV you will need to check it very carefully for spelling mistakes, grammar, and punctuation.

Get ahead!

Write down some examples of your skills that fall into the following categories:

- Problem solving
- Team work
- Practical skills
- Organizing.

Now write your CV, trying to include evidence of as many of these skills as possible. They are all things employers will like to see on your CV.

Melanie Thomas

Date of birth	13 January 1989
Address	79a East Avenue Cheltenham GL9 8IG
Telephone	01242 986 665
Email	mthomas@email.net
School	Upper Park School Cheltenham GL4 4KD 2000 - 2006

Make sure these are correct.

EDUCATION

Subject	**Qualification**	**Result**
Chemistry	A level	B
French	A level	C
Maths	A level	C
Art	GCSE	B
English	GCSE	C
French	GCSE	A
Geography	GCSE	C
German	GCSE	C
History	GCSE	D
Maths	GCSE	A
PE	GCSE	C
Science	GCSE	B

Put your most recent qualifications first.

Remember to include work experience.

EMPLOYMENT/WORK EXPERIENCE

Summer 2005 — Work experience (4 weeks) helping out with general office duties in a local civil engineering company.

INTERESTS

I am a member of the school drawing and design club.

Try to include relevant interests. Include any positions of responsibility, for example team captain.

REFEREE

Mr D Sprake
Form Teacher
Upper Park School
Cheltenham GL4 4KD

A teacher is a good person to use as a referee – make sure you ask their permission first.

above: *This is an example of the type of CV you could send out to employers.*

Covering letter

You should always send a handwritten or typed covering letter with your CV. This letter should explain why you are sending your CV and why you are applying for the job. You need to make your covering letter specific to the job you are applying for. Always address it to a specific person, never write "Dear Sir/Madam" (you may need to contact the organization by telephone to find out who to address it to). In your letter you should show that you know something about the company.

right: *A covering letter should look something like this.*

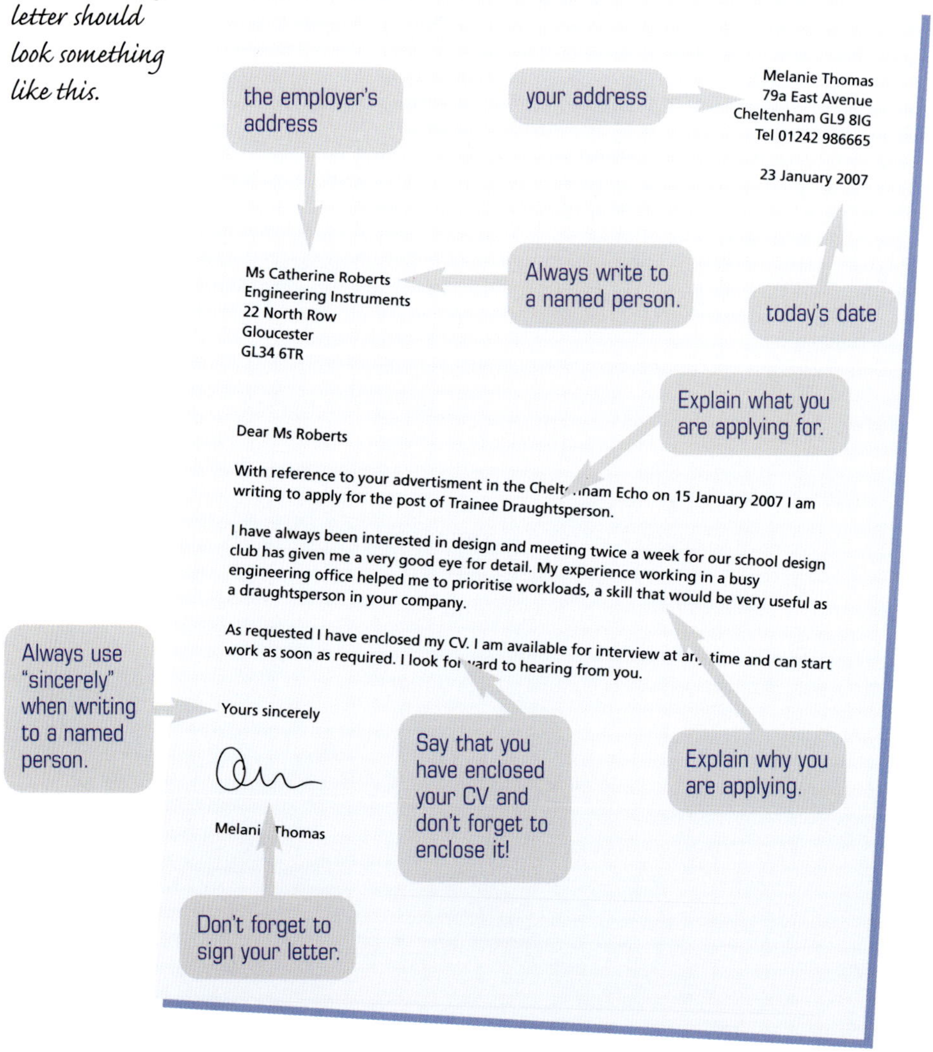
Melanie Thomas
79a East Avenue
Cheltenham GL9 8IG
Tel 01242 986665

23 January 2007

Ms Catherine Roberts
Engineering Instruments
22 North Row
Gloucester
GL34 6TR

Dear Ms Roberts

With reference to your advertisment in the Cheltenham Echo on 15 January 2007 I am writing to apply for the post of Trainee Draughtsperson.

I have always been interested in design and meeting twice a week for our school design club has given me a very good eye for detail. My experience working in a busy engineering office helped me to prioritise workloads, a skill that would be very useful as a draughtsperson in your company.

As requested I have enclosed my CV. I am available for interview at any time and can start work as soon as required. I look forward to hearing from you.

Yours sincerely

Melanie Thomas

Once you have sent off your CV or application form and covering letter, you have done all you can to impress the company from a distance. With any luck, it will lead to the next stage – a face-to-face interview.

The interview

Congratulations! You have sent off your CV or application form and have been invited to an interview. Do not celebrate too soon, though! Unfortunately a lot of other people will also have got this far. Employers interview a lot of people to try and find the best person for the job. You therefore have to show the interviewer that you are that person.

Before the interview

There are a number of things you can do to prepare yourself for an interview. The first thing you should do is find out everything you can about the company and what the job involves. You can even prepare some questions to ask the interviewer about the job. After all, the interview is also an opportunity for you to find out if you would like to work in that particular job or for that company. You should read through your application form or CV to remind yourself of how you answered any questions. The interviewer is bound to ask you questions related to the information you have given, so be prepared.

On the day of the interview, dress as smartly as you can. Make sure your appearance is neat and tidy. An employer will not be impressed if you have not made an effort with your appearance. Make sure you arrive for the interview 10 minutes early, so you will not be worried about being late.

At the interview

In the interview itself the most important thing to do is relax and be yourself. Be enthusiastic and answer all the questions clearly. If you do not understand a question ask the interviewer to explain it, and don't worry if you do not know the answer to every question you are asked. Just be honest and do not make things up ... a good interviewer will know when you are doing this. Remember to be positive and sell yourself.

Get ahead!

Think of answers to these questions before you go for an interview. They are the type of questions interviewers like to ask.

- Why do you want this job?
- Why do you think you would be good at this job?
- What are your strengths and weaknesses?

above: *At an interview, always be enthusiastic and honest.*

After the interview

When the interview is over, it is unlikely that you will find out if you got the job straight away. The company will usually have lots more people to interview before a decision is made. When you do get the result, do not give up if you have been unsuccessful, after all you may have come a close second. Ask the interviewer for feedback. This way you should be able to work out why you didn't get the job and will be able to do better next time.

Chapter 8

Onwards and upwards

Let us imagine that you have done well at school, obtained all the relevant qualifications, skills, and experience, applied for your ideal job in the engineering industry and been successful. Congratulations! So what happens now? How do you shape you career? What opportunities are there for further training and advancement?

Ongoing training while at work

As technology changes so quickly, engineers have to continue training so they can keep up with developments. Most employers will provide some form of on-the-job training when you start working for them. Once you are settled in your job there may be further opportunities to train at work, and you should take advantage of these. In order to do well in your chosen career, it is a good idea to get as much training as possible.

Engineering companies offer training at all levels. You are likely to receive a combination of in-house training (training offered by people in the same company), residential courses (for example, where you go on a course for a week), and distance learning (via email, most likely in your own time). In most engineering institutions, training will be an ongoing feature of your job, and you will be expected to keep up-to-date with new developments in your part of the industry.

Graduate trainees take part in a structured training programme for up to two years from when they start working. This training will be a combination of classroom teaching, on-the-job work experience, computer-based training and working alongside more senior staff. After completing this training and gaining enough experience, professional engineers may work towards chartered status (CEng). This is the highest professional status you can achieve.

CASE STUDY

Nitin is an engineering apprentice with a train company.

In the first year of my apprenticeship I was trained in the use of handheld tools so that I could undertake basic repair work and assist the craft engineers when necessary. I have a mentor, who is like a coach, and gives me extra training whenever I need it. I have also attended courses informing me about the latest developments on the railway system that may affect my work. Certificates are given for the successful completion of these courses.

above: *You will learn a lot from experienced colleagues at work.*

For most craft engineers and machine operators, training will be very much on the job. If you work for a small engineering firm, your training is likely to be broader than in a large firm, as you will be responsible for a wider range of activities.

Where do I go next?

Your prospects for promotion depend on your ability and performance in your job, as well as how ambitious you are. In the old days young people entering an engineering company worked their way up from the bottom, and probably stayed with that organization all their working lives. Today, if you begin your career as a machine operator and wish to move up the career ladder, you will need to gain additional qualifications and may need to move to a different company. It will all depend on where opportunities arise. But if you are prepared to work hard and keep moving you should be able to advance in your career.

With experience, opportunities for progression to more senior or managerial positions within the UK or abroad will become available. Engineering technicians can be promoted to technical engineers, who can move into management or **supervisory** roles. With experience, craft engineers can progress to supervisory roles, start their own business or take additional qualifications to progress to technician level.

Many types of engineers could also move into **consultancy** work or a different area of engineering. An experienced draughtsperson may be able to work on a **freelance** basis, working for companies who do not employ their own draughtsperson.

CASE STUDY

Brenda is an electronic engineer working for a large microchip company.

The first 4 or 5 years of work after you graduate are mostly spent gaining experience. After this there are two career options open to you. You can either follow a more senior technical route or move into management. Both of these have a standard promotion ladder, for example, you may move on to become a technical project leader or group manager. Some people decide to leave the company and go into consultancy work or start up their own companies.

People who succeed in the engineering industry develop a range of team-working and problem-solving skills that can also be useful in other jobs. Within the industry there are plenty of opportunities at all levels to develop an interesting career. However, there may come a time when you feel the need to move out of the industry, and these so-called "transferable skills" will enable you to do that.

Conclusion

So, are you still interested in pursuing a career in engineering? If you enjoy science, maths, and problem solving and are happy working in a team it could be the career for you.

A growing industry

The industry can certainly offer you a challenging and varied career, with plenty of opportunities for promotion and for making money. As we have seen, the skills of engineers are needed everywhere, and as such your skills will be in demand. The number of employers in the UK and abroad requiring your skills is on the increase due to the impact of new technology. Engineering is therefore an excellent area to be considering for a career.

left: *Engineer Jean Nouvel standing under the dome he designed for the Agbar Tower in Barcelona.*

Having said this, you need to think very carefully about what you want from your career. Engineering is not for everyone. Different people want different things, and the sooner you decide what type of engineering you want to do, the sooner you can start working towards gaining the relevant qualifications.

You also need to decide if you are the right person to enjoy working in this industry. You need to have the right personality and the right skills, as well as the right qualifications. And, as if this is not enough already, you will need to show some evidence that you are interested in a career in engineering, for example, through relevant work experience. Once you have thought carefully about all of this you will be well placed for applying for a job in the engineering industry. Then all you need to do is stand out from the crowd. Good luck!

below: *Keep up-to-date with all the latest advances by reading journals and magazines.*

Careers websites

Please note that qualifications and courses are subject to change.

- City and Guilds (www.city-and-guilds.co.uk)
  – This website tells you all about City and Guilds qualifications.
- Connexions Direct (www.connexions-direct.com)
  – A website that provides information and advice for young people, including learning and careers. It includes a link to the Jobs4U careers database.
- Learndirect (www.learndirect-advice.co.uk) and Learndirect Scotland (www.learndirectscotland.com/)
  – Go to "Careers", then "Job profiles", and select "Engineering".
- Modern Apprenticeships, Scotland (www.scottish-enterprise.com/modernapprenticeships)
  – Check out the case studies of people already training.
- Need2Know: Learning (www.need2know.co.uk/learning)
  – Information about studying and qualifications.
- Qualifications and Curriculum Authority (www.qca.org.uk/14-19)
  – Go to "Qualifications" and click on "Main qualification groups" to find out about NVQs.
- Scottish Vocational Qualifications (www.sqa.org.uk)
  – Find out all the latest qualifications information.
- The National Council for Work Experience (www.work-experience.org/)
  – Go to "Students and graduates" to search placements.

Get ahead in engineering and design!

- Institution of Chemical Engineers *(www.whynotchemeng.com)*
- Institution of Civil Engineers *(www.ice.org.uk)*
- Institution of Electrical Engineers *(www.iee.org.uk)*
- Institution of Mechanical Engineers *(www.imeche.org.uk)*
- Royal Aeronautical Society *(www.raes.org.uk)*
- The Engineering Careers Information Services *(www.enginuity.org.uk)*

A selection of jobs in the engineering industry

- Aeronautical engineer
- Agricultural engineer
- Aircraft technician
- Assembly operator
- Biomedical engineer
- Chemical engineer
- Civil engineer
- Design engineer
- Electrical engineer
- Electrical fitter
- Electronic engineer
- Heating and ventilating engineer
- Manufacturing engineer
- Marine engineer
- Materials engineer
- Mechanical engineer
- Petroleum engineer
- Project manager
- Propulsion engineer
- Quantity surveyor
- Technical assistant

Glossary

analytical able to examine something carefully and in great detail

assembly line system for making things in a factory where items move past a line of workers who each make or check one part of the item

chartered qualified by a professional association that has a royal charter (a document authorized by the Queen)

chemical engineering type of engineering that involves using chemicals to design and make new materials

circuit board piece of electrical equipment with a thin electrical cable connected to it that conducts electricity

civil engineering type of engineering that involves designing and building structures

code set of instructions that tells a computer what to do

Computer Aided Design (CAD) computer software that helps in the design of products and systems

consultancy business that gives expert professional advice

dam wall built across a river to stop it flowing

draughtsperson person who makes technical drawings

drawing board large flat board that engineers use to draw their designs

electrical engineering type of engineering that involves large scal electricity generation

electronic engineering type of engineering that involves small scal electricity generation

extracting taking things out of the ground, for example, minerals or oil

form the shape of something

freelance self-employed rather than working for a company

function the purpose of something

Higher National Certificate (HNC) technical qualification that you ca take after a National Certificate o after A-levels/Highers

Higher National Diploma (HND) technical qualification that you progress to from an HNC. It usual takes 2 years to achieve.

initiative ability to make your own decisions

internship training position within a company

lathe machine that shapes metal o wood by turning it round against a sharp tool

mechanical engineering type of engineering that involves designing and making machinery that has moving parts

Modern Apprenticeship qualification that enables you to work while you learn

microchip very small piece of electronic equipment used in computers and other electronic devices

National Vocational Qualification (NVQ) in England and Wales, a work-related, competence-based qualification that shows you have the knowledge and skills to do a job effectively. NVQs represent standards that are recognized by employers throughout the UK.

persuasive good at making other people agree with you

pharmaceutical making medicinal drugs

power tool tool that works using electricity

promotion move to a more important job in a company

prospectus booklet that advertises and describes courses at a university

robotic describes computer-controlled machines that do tasks for people

satellite electronic communication system in space

Scottish Vocational Qualification (SVQ) in Scotland, a work-related, competence-based qualification that shows you have the knowledge and skills to do a job effectively. SVQs represent standards that are recognized by employers throughout the UK.

supervisory role that involves directing and looking at the work of others

three-dimensional (3D) describes a structure that has length, depth, and height

Index

Titles in the *How to get ahead in* series include:

Hardback 978 1 4062 0442 1

Hardback 978 1 4062 0443 8

Hardback 978 1 4062 0440 7

Hardback 978 1 4062 0441 4

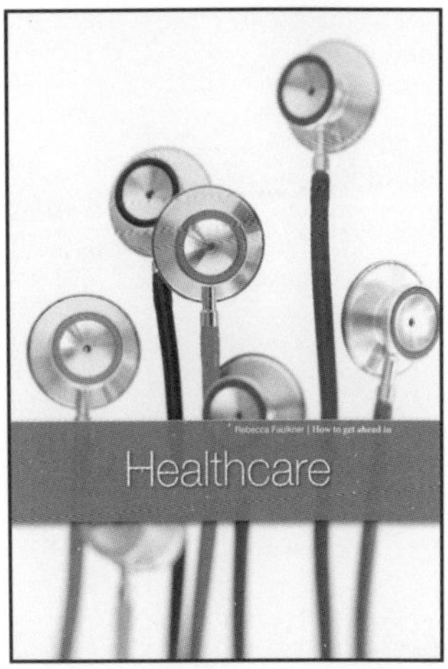

Hardback 978 1 4062 0444 5

Other titles available:

Armed and Civilian Forces	Hardback 978 1 4062 0450 6
Finance	Hardback 978 1 4062 0448 3
IT and Administration	Hardback 978 1 4062 0449 0
Leisure and Tourism	Hardback 978 1 4062 0447 6
Retail	Hardback 978 1 4062 0446 9

Find out about the other titles in this series on our website at www.raintreepublishers.co.uk